Original title:
Where the Roof Meets the Sky

Copyright © 2025 Creative Arts Management OÜ
All rights reserved.

Author: Jameson Hartfield
ISBN HARDBACK: 978-1-80587-133-0
ISBN PAPERBACK: 978-1-80587-603-8

Chasing Celestial Dreams

Up in the clouds, I lost my shoes,
I chased a comet, then got the blues.
A star told me jokes, but I wasn't impressed,
Fell flat on my face, more fun than rest.

I raced with the wind, ran circles so wide,
A balloon filled with dreams tried to take me for a ride.
But it popped with a laugh, left me in a knot,
Now I'm rope-jumping with an old astronaut!

Above the World's Edge

I built a ladder from dusty old books,
Climbed up to the moon with my funny looks.
Met a rabbit who wore a top hat and grin,
He offered me tea, said, 'Let the fun begin!'

We danced on the beams of a shimmering star,
Played hopscotch on Mars, it wasn't that far.
But when he started singing, my ears went on strike,
Next time I'll bring cookies, not a singing hick!

From Ground to Glory

With a pogo stick, I aimed for the sky,
But gravity giggled and made me fly high.
My neighbors looked up, saw my flailing spree,
Thought I was a bird, or at least a freaky bee.

I fell through a cloud, landed inside a pie,
A cherry explosion made my taste buds cry.
I shouted with joy, 'What a sweet, silly mess!'
Next time I'll invite them for a rooftop fest!

Peaks of Possibility

Scaling the peak with my oversized shoes,
Tripped on a rock and knocked over a moose.
He looked at me funny, then gave me a poke,
Said, 'Climbing like that, you're a real funny bloke!'

We started a club, 'The Wobbly and Wise,'
With meetings on cliffs, under shimmering skies.
There's laughter and cheese, and a dance called the flop,
Next stop is the clouds, but I think I might drop!

The Space Between

There's a realm up high, they say,
Where squirrels trade hats on a sunny day.
Clouds wear shoes, and rain drops climb,
Jokes echo back through the fabric of time.

Birds host parties, they flap and they twirl,
With each little chirp, they make feathers swirl.
A kite stole a taco from a passing cloud,
Laughter erupts, it's boisterous and loud.

Skylight Serenade

In the twilight where shadows tease,
Curious stars wear pajamas with ease.
The moon's juggling cheese, what a sight!
With crickets as fans, they cheer with delight.

A ship made of dreams floats by on a breeze,
Its captain shouts, 'Bring me flappy cheese!'
Planets dance salsa, dressed up in fun,
Twinkling bright, they're never outdone.

Dreams Amongst the Stars

A cat with a hat sits plotting a scheme,
To ride on a comet, fulfilling a dream.
Twinkling lights giggle, as they play tag,
With wishes in pockets, they're quite the ragtag.

Moonbeams throw raves, it's quite the affair,
While meteor showers turn into a fair.
Everyone's dancing, even the dust,
In this quirky place, we all can trust.

Gateway to High Places

In a world where ladders grow tall as the trees,
A penguin in sunglasses winks with a tease.
'Up here is a realm where no one is shy,'
He shoots for the stars, aiming high in the sky.

Flying fish boast with their shimmering scales,
While unicorns giggle and tell silly tales.
Each step on the cloud brings a burst of delight,
As rainbows shoot glitter, lighting up the night.

In Search of the Skies

I climbed atop a giant chair,
To glimpse the fluff, my views so rare.
A cloud waved back, said, "What's the deal?"
I laughed and thought, "Is this for real?"

In search of dreams, I lost my hat,
It floated past a curious cat.
It grinned and danced upon a breeze,
While I just searched for ways to tease.

The Unseen Threshold

I knocked upon a moonlit door,
A rabbit asked if I want more.
He said, "Your head's not in the game!"
I shrugged it off, it's kind of lame.

The trees above began to sway,
They whispered jokes about the day.
A squirrel piped up, "You're quite absurd!"
I laughed so hard, I lost my word.

Foundations of the Heavens

I wondered if the stars had feet,
Could they all dance to a funky beat?
I offered them a slice of pie,
They giggled, flinging crumbs up high.

A comet zoomed, forgot to stop,
It crashed into a candy shop.
The lollipops flew, oh what a sight,
I chuckled loud, 'Now that's delight!'

Skylines of the Soul

I tried to paint the sky so blue,
But ended up with every hue.
The sun just laughed, then called me skilled,
I blushed and thought, 'My dreams are filled!'

A bird flew past, said with a grin,
"Life's a joke, so let's begin!"
I tossed my brush and danced around,
With colors splashed, I'm glory-bound!

Horizons Whispering Secrets

Clouds sit like cotton, cozy and round,
Pigeons gossip while hopping the ground.
Stars wink at strangers, a wink and a grin,
Daydreaming kittens, where mischief begins.

Sunsets like pop tarts, frosted in gold,
The wind tells tall tales that never get old.
Umbrellas dance salsa in rain's little spree,
And raincoats are capes for the brave and the free.

Nuances of the Celestial Vault

The moon's in pajamas, just lounging in beams,
Shooting stars laugh at our wildest dreams.
A comet trips over its own tail so bright,
While crickets compose symphonies deep in the night.

Jellybeans float by with a giggle and twirl,
Wishing wells chuckle with every whirl.
The sky plays hopscotch with clouds in a race,
As laughter echoes in the vast open space.

Framework of Skyward Aspirations

Kites flirt with breezes, soaring so high,
While rainbows sip tea with a sparkly sigh.
Grasshoppers jump in a whimsical tune,
And squirrels steal snacks to share with the moon.

Balloons have a party, just floating around,
They bounce to the music, no care for the ground.
Lightbulbs of wishes illuminate the scene,
As giggling stars wink, feeling so keen.

Veils of Mist Above the Peaks

Fog wears a tutu, swirling with grace,
Mountains don sombreros, up in their place.
A yodeling echo joins in for the fun,
While marmots play tag, always on the run.

Sunflowers gossip about bees and their flights,
As daisies debate who shines brightest at nights.
Clouds have a picnic, sharing puffs of delight,
In the whimsical world, where all's just right.

Celestial Glimpses and Grounded Hearts

A chicken flew up, thought it could soar,
But landed headfirst, right in a store.
The clerk looked bemused, as it squawked with glee,
"I just wanted snacks, not a spot on TV!"

Balloons drifted high, in a dance of delight,
While a dog barked loudly, trying to take flight.
He leaped and he bounced, with a whimsical twist,
And chased clouds above, none could resist!

Pinnacle of Reflection and Reverie

A squirrel in sunglasses, lounging on a tree,
Claimed it was 'fashion', not just for a spree.
He posed for a pic, with a nut in his hand,
"I'm a model of nature, just look how I stand!"

An ant with a helmet marched with great pride,
"I'm leading my army!" he boldly replied.
But tripped on a leaf, oh, what a grand flop,
"I'll regroup and restart, but first, I need to hop!"

The Dance of Shade and Light

A shadow tried dancing, but stumbled around,
Tripped on a rock and fell flat on the ground.
"This groove is hard!" it announced to the sun,
"Next time, let's tango; I'm just not the one!"

The sun chuckled softly, casting golden beams,
While a cat in a hammock drifted in dreams.
"We can chill, my friend, no need for a race,
Just swing with the breeze, and let's find our place!"

Ascendancy in the Colorful Expanse

A kite flew too high, got tangled in trees,
"I am not stuck!" it cried, grasping for ease.
A bird chirped with envy, quite stuck in its nest,
"I wanted that freedom; you're such a pest!"

Down below, a toddler pointed and squealed,
"Look at the colors!" as laughter revealed.
He tossed up some glitter, launched it with flair,
"Now all of the world sparkles beyond compare!"

The Touch of the Infinite

A cow jumped high, as cows tend to do,
Landing on clouds, laughing, 'Look at my view!'
With a swing of her tail, she tap-danced on air,
All the sheep below, just asking, 'Is it fair?'

The grass started giggling, the trees took a bow,
One squirrel cried out, 'Is this a new cow?'
She winked with a grin, said, 'I'm part of the crew!'
Then floated away, saying, 'Catch me if you can, too!'

Lifting the Veil of Day

The sun yawned wide, stretched out its bright arms,
Tickling the rooftops, spreading its charms.
A rooster chimed in with a laugh and a crow,
'Wake up, sleeping sloths! It's time for the show!'

The walls joined the dance, shimmying with flair,
As curtains swung open, revealing fresh air.
Lamps winked at the shadows, making them twirl,
The world had awakened, in a bright, crazy swirl!

Starlit Traces

Stars in the night jumped in playful glee,
Playing tag with the moon, just like you and me.
They tumbled and spun through the velvet blue skies,
While dreaming of donuts in sweet, sugary pies.

One star took a dive, making a splash,
The universe giggled, a magical crash!
With comets as friends, they painted the dark,
Creating a mural—cosmic art! What a lark!

The Upper Realm

Up high on the hill, where the breezes abound,
The squirrels debated who'd conquer the ground.
One claimed a crown made of twigs, just so neat,
While the birds laughed aloud, flapping their feet.

A raccoon came strolling, his pie-eyed delight,
Grinning at chaos that danced with the night.
They argued and pranced, full of zest and good cheer,
In a realm full of nonsense—oh, let's all be here!

Constellations of Hope

Stars giggle in the dark,
They dance around a lark.
Wishing on a playful star,
They wonder how they got this far.

A comet zooms with flair,
Did it lose its way in the air?
Bright ideas twinkle and shine,
Like dreams that clink in a glass of wine.

Clouds wear pajamas, fluffy and white,
Having pillow fights each night.
They block the moon with a wink,
And giggle as the stars all think.

Planets tease in a cosmic race,
Rolling with laughter, they keep pace.
With a wink, they drop a line,
In the galaxy's joke book, so divine.

Through the Atmosphere

Balloons float like dreams gone free,
Whispering secrets to a bumblebee.
They laugh and twist on the breeze,
Promising the air to always please.

Kites are soaring too high, they say,
Chasing clouds that just want to play.
A gust of wind, oh how it tricks,
Launching them into aerial flips.

A plane honks like a friendly goose,
As it sails through a smoky juice.
Passengers giggle in their seats,
Jokes flying faster than their feats.

Frogs on rooftops croak in delight,
Hoping the stars will see their light.
Jumping up to catch a spark,
Finding joy before it gets dark.

Rings of the Sky

Saturn spins with a goofy grin,
Its rings are filled with cosmic sin.
Like hula hoops in an alien dance,
Riding the waves of space's chance.

Jupiter's storms swirl and toss,
It's a party where no one's lost.
They throw confetti made of gas,
Bouncing around in a jolly class.

Stars wear boots and take big steps,
On a galactic course for mischief reps.
Each twinkle a giggle from afar,
Making wishes on a shooting star.

A playful breeze whispers notes,
To the planets in stylish coats.
In this sky, there's laughter galore,
Even the sun can't help but roar.

Ascending Wishes

Up, up with a kite so bright,
Balloons rise to dizzying heights.
They scamper past a blushing moon,
In a sky that sings an airy tune.

Wishes float on fluffy clouds,
Chasing dreams and giggling crowds.
Inflatable hearts bounce and sway,
Sharing secrets as they drift away.

The rockets are dressed in silly hats,
Honking like enthusiastic brats.
They zoom past stars that dance and cheer,
Shooting for giggles, never fear.

So here's to wishes that soar and glide,
On the winds, where laughter's wide.
In the realm above, fun fills the air,
With every chuckle, we're all a pair.

Breath of the Beyond

Up here, I can almost dance,
Wobbling in a bright blue trance.
A cloud's my hat, a star my tie,
Who knew I'd sprout these wings to fly?

The eggs I dropped were not the same,
They scrambled up to join my game.
Just watch them spin and do the twist,
In this bizarre sky, they can't resist.

Bees buzz by with jokes to share,
Humming tunes without a care.
I giggle at their tiny plight,
As flowers bloom in pure delight.

Forget your worries, take a look,
The world's a giant picture book.
Just don't forget, when fall comes near,
To keep your shoes on, or disappear!

The Sky's Embrace

Clouds tickle my unruly hair,
As I surge through the evening air.
I ask the sun to lend me light,
To sneak a wink from day to night.

The birds laugh loud, they're in on it,
Spreading tales of a weather fit.
A breeze swoops by with playful tease,
Whispering secrets among the trees.

My shoes are lost; they floated high,
Chasing dreams of flying pie.
The moon beams down with a cheeky grin,
"Let's play hide-and-seek, come on in!"

So here I drift, with joy to share,
In this blue bowl, without a care.
We giggle, we wiggle, in cosmic glee,
In a world where fun is wild and free!

Awakening to Altitudes

Waking up where dreams take flight,
In pajamas, I soar, what a sight!
My neighbor's goat has joined the spree,
Doing yoga, oh can't you see?

The sun's a jester, bright and bold,
Throwing funny shadows—can you behold?
While squirrels giggle at my plight,
As I trip on air in pure delight.

We float on waffles, syrup thick,
A happy dance, a quirky trick.
Life's a bowl of frosted fun,
Up in these heights under the sun.

So if you see me twirling wide,
Just wave hello, and set aside.
For laughter echoes in the air,
In this world where joy is rare!

Reaching for the Eternal

I reached for stars, they laughed and danced,
With a wink, they spun, they pranced.
"Come join our party, oh don't be shy,
We've got confetti from the sky!"

The sun wore shades, and gave a nod,
While dancing with the restless plod.
In the air, a trumpet's blast,
As cotton candy clouds drift past.

"Don't forget to bring your snacks!"
Called out a comet with golden tracks.
Lost in this frolic, I forget my woes,
As peanuts rain from shooting shows.

Here up high, the fun won't cease,
With silky breezes, I find my peace.
As laughter ripples through the night,
I reach for dreams with pure delight!

Elevation of Spirit and Realm

On high, I toast to fluff, a cloud,
With dreams like balloons, I laugh out loud.
A squirrel swings by, wearing a hat,
Does he think he's a king or just a spazz?

Cereal bowls swirl in the air's embrace,
While raindrops dance, a slippery race.
I wonder if trees gossip, oh dear!
Whispering secrets that only they hear.

Kites tug at strings, demanding a thrill,
Drifting on winds that roam at will.
A pigeon slides by with a questionable style,
Is he strutting for birds, or just for a while?

Yet up here, the air has its own quirks,
Gravity's just a suggestion, it lurks.
With giggles galore and the clouds out of sight,
It seems, oh my friend, we're flying tonight.

Encounters with the Infinite Firmament

I met a star that stole my drink,
It winked as if to say, 'Let's rethink.'
We played checkers on an asteroid's edge,
While space cats cheered and formed a pledge.

The moon tried stand-up, cracked a few jokes,
I nearly fell off my glow-in-the-dark folks.
Each punchline sailed past like a comet's tail,
As laughter soared high in the cosmic trail.

Planets spun 'round, having a ball,
While meteors raced, it was quite the crawl.
A black hole whispered, 'Lose the frown,'
I said, 'Can you take me to the nearest town?'

With a grin and a wiggle, I danced with the sky,
Funny how gravity just lets it fly.
In this odd space, with no need to adhere,
Encounters abound, the cosmos is near.

Symphony of Hues Above

A rainbow tickles the tips of my shoes,
Its colors are cheerful, like jolly good news.
A bluebird croons a silly old tune,
While dumbfounded clouds just puff and swoon.

Orange giggles ripple in evening's glow,
As purple drags green for a fun frolic show.
The sun throws confetti on everyone down,
And the horizon blushes like a clown.

Birds don't play fair in this vibrant spree,
With each note they warble, it's pure glee.
A painted sky laughs as shadows collide,
In this carnival of light, we take a ride.

So join the parade of joy up above,
Where laughter and colors fit like a glove.
As the stars pop out with a wink and a sigh,
We dance in the hues of the vast painted sky.

Echoes Amongst the Ether

An echo bounced high, seeking a friend,
It called out my name, 'Let's giggle and blend!'
The clouds joined in, a marshmallow crew,
With fluffs and puffs, they know what to do.

Voices of comets sing silly refrains,
While meteors chuckle, 'Oh, isn't it plain?'
The universe whispers, 'Jump in the fun!'
As laughter and stardust dance just like one.

With each silly shout from the depths of the dark,
I swear I saw Saturn do a pink spark.
Venus rolled over, her laughter a breeze,
While planets played hopscotch with grace and ease.

In this wild ether, let's bounce and let's play,
For each wacky echo brightens the day.
From giggling orbits to whimsical sights,
We find all our joy in these starry delights.

Veil of the Atmosphere

In a world where clouds play tag,
And dreams float like a friendly rag,
I tried to jump and touch a plume,
But ended up in a garden bloom.

The sun winks like a cheeky sprite,
While kites dance with all their might,
I wave to birds in fancy suits,
Hope they won't ask for my best boots.

Breezes tickle my upturned nose,
As squirrels juggle acorns, I suppose,
I laugh as they plot their next prank,
While I just wish I had a crank.

With each laugh, I reach for more,
Chasing laughter like it's a score,
The sky's my stage, I dance and spin,
In this place where silliness wins!

The Skyline's Embrace

I climbed a ladder made of dreams,
To ride the skyline's quirky beams,
Each rooftop holds a secret tale,
Of dancing cats and a barking snail.

The moon hung low, a cheese so bright,
I thought I'd take a daring bite,
But found my face stuck in a tree,
Who knew a squirrel would disagree?

The stars giggle in their twinkly cheer,
As I balance with no hint of fear,
But gravity chuckles, it gets me back,
To a soft landing—a gentle whack.

With every jump, I let out a grin,
For laughter is where my fun begins,
The nights are wild, full of delight,
As the skyline whispers, 'What a sight!'

Infinity Above

I reached for the heavens, a curious quest,
In spaghetti storms, I was quite a mess,
With spaghetti in my hair, I did declare,
That pasta's good if you take it up there!

Clouds turned into fluffy beds,
Where dreams float 'round in funny threads,
A bear in pajamas waved goodbye,
As I asked the stars for a slice of pie.

The moon wore a hat, sidewise, of course,
As I flew by on a frisbee horse,
Laughter echoed in the cosmic spree,
While planets laughed as they spun at tea.

So in this space, I jiggled and danced,
While comets rolled their eyes, entranced,
The infinity above is witty and spry—
I'm never alone, just reach for the sky!

Reflections of the Firmament

In puddles, I see a bouncing star,
Wearing rubber boots, not too far,
As I jump, splashes fly with glee,
Giggling reflections, just me and me.

A wise old cloud said, 'Don't look down!'
But I tripped over a soft, fluffy frown,
It chuckled at my silly fall,
As other clouds joined in the brawl.

The sunset painted all in haste,
As if it was cooking a vibrant feast,
With each glow, it turned more bright,
The sky threw sparkles, what a sight!

The firmament dances above so sly,
With whispers and giggles, it floats by,
And I join in the whimsical cheer,
In this silly place where joy is clear!

Horizons of the Heart

In the land of dreams, we sketched a tale,
With squirrels in bow ties, on a giant whale.
They danced on clouds, sprouted wings of glee,
Each dive a splash in the cup of tea.

At sunrise, we feasted on pancakes tall,
The syrup flowed like a waterfall.
We rode on llamas wearing hats so bright,
Chasing rainbows, oh what a sight!

On kite-fights, we soared in the zephyrs,
Our jokes got tangled like shoelace shifters.
The sun winked cheekily, the moon gave a grin,
While the stars played hopscotch, let the games begin!

So raise a toast to the odd and the weird,
To every child's giggle that we have cheered.
In this land of whimsy, where laughter will start,
Adventure awaits on the horizons of heart.

Celestial Threshold

Under the arch of a cotton candy sky,
I tripped on stardust, oh my! oh my!
A llama with glasses pointed out the moon,
Said it dances nightly to a catchy tune.

Juggling pancakes, a chef from Mars,
Flipped them like UFOs, leaving greasy scars.
Shoelaces untied, I took a big leap,
Fell into a universe of giggles and sheep.

Comets as buses, let's take a ride,
With disco balls and confetti inside.
Sat on the edge, with my feet dangling free,
On a swing made of whispers, just you and me.

At the celestial gate, with a wink and a smile,
We signed a contract for laughter and style.
Life is a circus, full of cheer and grace,
On this threshold, we'll make a funny face!

Peaks of Ambition

Scaling the heights of ridiculous schemes,
With bears in tutus, fulfilling our dreams.
A waterfall flows with chocolate delight,
And we climb up high on a swing made of light.

In the summit of giggles, we set our sights,
On balloon animals fighting in kite flights.
A cheeky chimp serenades with a song,
While the sun rolls its eyes, saying, 'Come along!'

With pickles for sparks, we ignite our goals,
Hearts full of laughter, we conquer the rolls.
The view from the top is a sight to behold,
With candy-coated dreams, and stories retold.

So raise your glass to ambitions so bright,
In a world full of whimsy, we take to flight.
On these peaks of delight, we'll always find cheer,
For humor is mighty, and joy is our steer.

Boundless Above

Under a sky made of quirky delight,
We danced with the breezes, grinning at height.
With fish in tuxedos, we zoomed on a plane,
Sipping lemonade while playing a game.

Kites with big smiles sailed into the blue,
Painted in splashes of every hue.
Juggling our hopes on a tightrope of glee,
A trampoline friendship, how bouncy could we be?

The sun wore sunglasses, feeling so cool,
While clouds played charades, defining their rule.
In this boundless expanse of laughter so pure,
With a sprinkle of joy that we all can assure.

So join in the dance beneath these broad spans,
Where joy knows no limits, and laughter expands.
With whimsy as our guide, we'll soar and explore,
Above and beyond, oh, the fun we'll adore!

Between Earth and the Infinite

Up high I float with my bag of cheese,
Chasing butterflies on a gentle breeze.
A squirrel sits down, offers me a snack,
Says, 'You should try, it's quite a whack!'

Staring at clouds that look like pies,
Creating desserts for hungry skies.
The sun waves hello, a cheeky grin,
While I wonder how to fit my cat in.

A bird sings songs of silly old lore,
Perched on my head like a feathery door.
I wink at the stars with a goofy glare,
And they nod back, with a twinkle and flair.

Gravity laughs, pulling me down,
As I tumble, pretending to frown.
Floating again, just like a kite,
In the land where laughter takes flight!

Clouds as Canvases

In the art of fluff, we paint with glee,
A canvas of clouds for you and me.
Swirls of cotton, with splashes of blue,
I think I just saw a donut, too!

A giraffe pokes its head from a marshmallow hill,
As rain puffs laugh, they've had their fill.
A dragon zooms past, tail made of cream,
Eating the sun, or so it would seem.

Jelly-bean raindrops fall from above,
Dancing in joy, like a silly love.
Imagination runs wild and free,
On this whimsical journey, just you and me.

We sketch silly shapes, a duck with a tie,
As the birds join in, they flutter and fly.
Art in the air, what a funny sight,
Who knew that clouds could bring such delight!

Summit of Whispers

Atop the heights where thoughts run grand,
Whispers of goats take a quirky stand.
'Look! A mountain! Twirling with glee,
We've got the best view, just wait and see!'

Up here, the air is a giggly tease,
Tickling noses and shaking knees.
The trees start to dance, oh what a show,
With squirrels as dancers, stealing the flow.

A balloon floats by, wearing a smile,
I think it's been drifting for quite a while.
It yells, "Join the party, let's all just play!"
While chipmunks chime in, "Please stay, hooray!"

The mountain hums an old goofy tune,
As I laugh with the stars, under the moon.
In this place where whispers turn to cheer,
Every joke's a treasure, every laugh sincere!

The View from Above

Up high, I see a circus on the ground,
With acrobats flipping, around and around.
A peanut-shaped plane buzzes with glee,
Its pilot's a dog, sipping on sweet tea!

People below, wearing hats made of cake,
Dance to the rhythm, make no mistake.
While cows wear sunglasses, lounging with style,
I've never seen fashion like this in a while.

The cat's in a hammock, snoozing away,
While dreams take flight on this sunny day.
What a sight! A parade made of cheese,
I can't stop laughing, my heart's at ease.

From my lofty perch, the world seems absurd,
Laughter floats up, undisturbed.
In this whimsical realm, oh what a thrill,
Every glance a joy, every moment a chill!

Celestial Borders and Earthly Cradles

Up above the clouds, they play,
An acorn dreams of flying one day.
It wears a tiny aviator hat,
And thinks it's cooler than a fat Cheshire cat.

The sun throws paint on the rooftops bright,
While pigeons strut like they own the night.
A squirrel is plotting to take over the view,
With plans that include a grand parade, too.

Winds whisper secrets, silly and sweet,
And clouds argue over who has the best seat.
A ladybug joins, claiming she's queen,
In a kingdom of whimsy, where everything's green.

So raise a toast to those lofty dreams,
To acorns that fly with imaginary beams.
For laughter dances where night skies reside,
And all that we wish seems to take us for a ride.

Airy Trails of Unimagined Journeys

In a box of wishes, the dreams take flight,
With jellybean pilots feeling just right.
They zoom past the moon on a rainbow plane,
Screaming with glee, 'We're insane! We're insane!'

A dandelion puff joined the crew,
With its flight path drawn in sparkling dew.
It twirled and it twirled, like it was on a spree,
While ants cheered, 'We'll be the travel agency!'

They landed on stars, oh what a delight,
Where marshmallow bunnies had tea every night.
A comet swung low to share its sweet treats,
While giggles erupted like pop-pop popcorn eats.

So if you're ever feeling quite stuck,
Grab your own jellybeans and don't be a schmuck.
For laughter is magic that runs on the trails,
Of dreams unencumbered, where humor prevails.

Above the Eaves

A cat with a cape sits high on the roof,
Sipping cocoa while making a spoof.
He claims he's a hero on a noble quest,
To find the warm sun, he thinks he knows best.

The chimney squeaks, 'Are you serious, mate?'
While the weather vane twirls, feeling great.
Beneath a blanket of stars, they conspire,
To create silly tales that never tire.

A dreamer's hot air balloon quite defies,
The traffic reports of the pigeons' lies.
It wobbles and giggles, a sight to behold,
Askew in the wind, like a story retold.

As the night drips laughter, the moon starts to snore,
Jokes get thrown like confetti galore.
For in this high home, fun's the decree,
Above the eaves, where we're all wild and free.

Ascent to Infinity

With socks on their heads, they hiked up a tree,
Seekers of wisdom and wild jubilee.
The branches bowed low, squeaking their glee,
As squirrels looked on, wondering, 'Who's that crazy we?'

A ladder made of marshmallows climbed high,
While gummy bears wondered how they would fly.
The wisdom spoke clear in a wobbly voice,
'This is the realm of the silly, rejoice!'

Clouds wore sunglasses, chilling in style,
As birds told corny jokes that made time worthwhile.
Each hiccup from laughter rattled the sky,
Bringing stars down to hear the next silly sigh.

So venture forth, to that topsy-turvy place,
Where silliness reigns, and joy finds its space.
The ascent to infinity starts with a grin,
A journey of laughter, let the fun begin!

The Quiet Ascent

In a world where the ladders grow,
I climbed to heights I never know.
Pigeons laughed, they called me a fool,
Why dance with clouds? I'm a ground-bound jewel.

Atop this perch, I sip my tea,
And wave to squirrels, they glance at me.
A breeze tickled my silly hat,
I bowed to the wind, imagine that!

Each puff of air, a balloon's delight,
As I juggle dreams into the night.
The sun rolled by, a golden ball,
Hey, come back here, don't you dare fall!

Yet here I dwell, beneath the blue,
Where giggles sprout, just like morning dew.
With birds for jesters and clouds for friends,
I laugh at the sky, 'cause the fun never ends!

Zephyrs of Desire

Oh, to dance with breezes, light and spry,
I twirl through dreams, oh my, oh my!
Gusts whisper secrets, mischievous tunes,
While I chase sunshine and bounce off moons.

In my balloon shoes, I leap so high,
Trying to catch a cloud that winked by.
"Come down!" they giggle, "It's quite a show!"
I tumbled past rainbows, oh what a glow!

On airships built of pies and cakes,
We soared through starlight, such crazy breaks!
A comet swooshed by, wearing a hat,
It yelled, "Why not? Let's make some chit-chat!"

So here I float, in a caper so bold,
With zephyrs of wishes and stories untold.
Together we laugh, spinning in glee,
In this whimsical dance, so wild and free!

Brilliance Above

Up in the ether, I spot a gleam,
The sun's bright joke, it's quite the theme.
Stars with glasses adjust their sights,
As I hiccup with laughter at cosmic heights.

I met a comet, braided with gold,
Said, "Let's have tea, after stories are told."
We sipped on starlight, oh, what a brew!
"Pass the space biscuits," I joyfully blew.

A galaxy twirled, it lost its place,
"Oops! I'm a little too far, just keep up the pace."
I played hopscotch on Saturn's rings,
Humming away, as the universe sings.

So when you look up at this shimmering show,
Remember the laughter that freely will flow.
For brilliance above holds the happiest cheer,
In the cosmic dance, we've nothing to fear!

Driftwood in the Clouds

On fluffy logs, we journey with glee,
Driftwood afloat, set wild and free.
Clouds form sofas, fluffy and wide,
As we giggle, toss and glide.

I saw a whale with a party hat,
Doing the cha-cha, oh fancy that!
"Join the fun!" it did loudly call,
As a flying fish pranced, oh, what a ball!

Kites turned to puppies, woofing away,
Let's fetch the sun, in a playful display.
The moon winked down, a knowing smile,
"Stay a bit longer, let's linger awhile."

So here in the clouds, we swirl and play,
With driftwood laughter lighting the day.
A silly adventure, above all things,
In this whimsical realm, oh, how joy sings!

A Dance with the Stars

Up on the hill, my dog wears a hat,
Barking at orbs—what's up with that?
I twirl with the planets, they giggle and sway,
While meteors dance in a cosmic ballet.

The moon's doing the limbo, how low can she go?
I can almost hear her say, "Let's steal the show!"
Stars wink like mischief, with laughter so bright,
As we jig and we jive through the velvety night.

A comet hops over—I'm caught in its beam,
With each outrageous move, I'm living the dream.
Gravity's joking, it's losing its grip,
I'm flying with laughter, on this stellar trip.

In the end, I tip my hat to the night,
To the dance of the celestial, a glorious sight.
With my furry friend laughing, we wave goodbye,
As the universe giggles, and we float on high.

The Final Horizon

On the edge of the world, where the ground takes a leap,
I wore a silly hat, made of chicken and sheep.
Birds are applauding, they're flapping with glee,
As I attempt to balance a cat on my knee.

I shout to the mountains, "You can't bring me down!"
They chuckle in echoes, wearing old-fashioned crowns.
A sky full of dreams, and clouds made of fluff,
I'm tumbling through giggles—this life is so tough!

I build my own rocket, from spoons and some twine,
With a sprinkle of laughter, it's destined to shine.
The countdown is silly, three, two, or maybe one,
But I launch into chuckles, oh, look at me run!

The final horizon whispers secrets so bright,
As I soar through the cosmos, full of delight.
With a wink and a nudge, I greet the unknown,
In a land full of laughter, I'm never alone.

Echoes of Altitude

Above the clouds, there's a squirrel in a tie,
Preaching big ideas, while munching on pie.
I chuckle so hard, my breath turns to mist,
As I join his odd meeting, I can't resist.

The air is a giggle, it tickles my nose,
As butterflies dance in their fanciest clothes.
I shout to the sun, "Hey, brighten my day!"
And he shines in a bowtie, all yellow and gay.

With each echo that bounces from mountain to hill,
I'm spinning in circles, I can't sit still.
Altitude's calling with a whimsical rhyme,
As clouds throw a party, it's funny time!

Later, I'll tumble to the earth in a swoop,
But for now, I'm a part of this ridiculous group.
With laughter like fireworks lighting the sky,
I dance with the echoes, oh my, oh my!

Bridging the Vastness

In a bridge made of giggles, I glide on a beam,
With marshmallows bobbing, it's just like a dream.
The stars throw confetti, while I tiptoe with flair,
On a road paved with laughter, oh, nothing compares!

A giraffe with a monocle joins in my quest,
He says with a chuckle, "We're simply the best!"
We stretch through the sky, bridging puffs of delight,
As the universe chuckles at our silly flight.

With each step I take, the cosmos will sway,
While comets do pirouettes, showing the way.
Creativity dances in this fantastic scene,
As I stumble on stardust, feeling so keen.

At the end of the bridge, there's a great big grin,
Where the laughter erupts, and the fun can begin.
I skip back to earth with a heart full of cheer,
In a world that's so vast, what a joy to be here!

Beyond the Known

Up high where the pigeons play,
And squirrels have much to say.
A cat thinks he's King of the Hill,
While daylight offers its thrill.

The clouds are just cotton candy,
Floating dreams that seem quite dandy.
A kite takes off with a giggle,
While children below jump and wiggle.

Adventures soar, no plan to chart,
In this realm, there's room to start.
Chasing shadows, laughing loud,
Every whim embraced, unbowed.

With spaghetti falling from above,
And donuts raining down, oh love!
In this place where jesters are free,
Life dances with delight, you see!

Tethered to Dreams

Balloons tied to a hat so bright,
Floating high with sheer delight.
A dog in a cape, what a sight!
He thinks he's off to take flight.

The moon winks, a partner in crime,
While stars giggle, keeping time.
As penguins race on tiny cars,
The night swells with laughter from afar.

As taffy clouds stretch and curl,
A rainbow dances, gives a twirl.
In a world of silly delights,
We leap around on merry heights.

To reach for dreams like candy skies,
Where giggles echo, laughter flies.
Each moment a joke, a cute tease,
In this land of whimsy, we're at ease!

Airborne Echoes

Bats in tuxedos take to flight,
Dancing under the moonlight bright.
A sandwich waves and starts to glide,
While flying fish swim with pride.

Giggles bounce from tree to tree,
As squirrels plan their comedy spree.
An owl hoots a laugh or two,
In this show, we all have a view.

The breeze tickles, sends hats away,
As we shout for the sky's cabaret.
Laughter floats, a curious tune,
As butterflies join, a colorful swoon.

With pies that fall, and laughter's wing,
We float on joy, as echoes sing.
In this circus where chaos is king,
Every event makes our hearts spring!

The Height of Possibility

Up above, pancakes take flight,
Flipping upside down, what a sight!
A giraffe in boots twirls in glee,
In this world, anything can be.

Socks that dance from fence to wall,
Until they land in a silly sprawl.
An ant wearing shades sips sweet tea,
While clouds play hopscotch carefree.

Lemonade fountains sprinkle fun,
As sunset races towards the sun.
The laughter spreads, a zany trend,
In this place, where rules won't bend.

So join the jesters, take a leap,
In dreams that run, and never sleep.
With hearts that soar and spirits high,
This is the hub where giggles fly!

Skylines and Stardust

In a city with towers so tall,
I wondered if they might fall.
The pigeons are plotting, I see,
Above my coffee, oh me!

The lights twinkle like stars in a joke,
While taxis honk like a silly folk.
The skyline's a painter's big laugh,
Each building a quirky photo graph.

I waved to a cloud, it waved back too,
We giggled around like the sun's funny crew.
The sunsets drop candy from above,
In a world full of whimsy and love.

So let's dance with the shadows, my friend,
As the city giggles and the day begins to end.
We'll twirl with the gales, under bright moons,
And laugh with the stars, like we're old cartoons.

Wind's Serenade at Day's End

The wind sings songs of a playful breeze,
I giggle at leaves spinning with ease.
A squirrel out-scurries a curious cat,
In a duel of silliness, imagine that!

Chasing shadows on the path we roam,
The setting sun is our funny home.
It winks and whispers, 'Come dance with me!'
While clouds become pillows, oh what glee!

The crickets join in, with their bug-like band,
Creating a tune that's simply grand.
We dance on the grass, twirling with flair,
Each footfall giggles; it's quite the affair.

As stars peek out, the night plays coy,
Even the moon cannot help but enjoy.
So laugh with the dusk, let your heart be light,
In this symphony of night, everything's bright!

Canvas of Clouds and Wishes

Above the trees and over the hills,
The clouds paint pictures, giving us thrills.
A rabbit hops high, then vanishes fast,
In a world where the dreams and shapes are cast.

Each puff of white is a joke on the go,
Who would've thought clouds could put on a show?
They dance like experts in a funny parade,
While rainbows throw confetti, a lovely charade.

I asked a cloud if it could stay,
It giggled and floated, then drifted away.
A raindrop fell softly, right on my nose,
"Oops!" laughed the heavens, a ticklish prose.

Wishes hang low on the pastel sky,
Like the dreams of a child that makes you sigh.
So let's sketch our laughter, doodles, and cheer,
In this canvas of clouds, where nothing's unclear!

The Place of Outstretched Dreams

In a garden of giggles, where dreams collide,
We swing with the stars, what a whimsical ride!
A tickle from Jupiter, a wink from the moon,
We'll dance with the comets, morning, noon!

The grass whispers secrets of wishes so bright,
While daisies laugh softly in the warm light.
I chased a butterfly wearing a bow,
But it fluttered away, oh no, oh no!

With laughter like bubbles, we soar in the air,
Each heartbeat a rhythm, a song rare and fair.
We pluck at the laughter, letting it fly,
In this garden of wonder, our hopes touch the sky.

As night wraps us gently, we'll dream and we'll scheme,
Of the place where our giggles can stretch and redeem.
For here in this realm, we're delightfully free,
In a world of outstretched dreams, just you and me!

Mapping the Infinite

I set my sights on distant stars,
With a map that's drawn on candy bars.
Navigating puddles like cosmic pools,
Laughing at the upside-down gravity rules.

I asked a bird for directions once,
It just flapped away like a dodgy dunce.
A squirrel pointed with a nutty grin,
Said, "Head to the tree, that's where I've been!"

My compass spins, a dizzy dream,
Chasing comets that sprout whipped cream.
I think I'd rather just roam and play,
Than chase some stars that dart away.

So here I stand, with a grin so wide,
Planning journeys with squirrels as guides.
With laughter echoing through the night,
Mapping the infinite, what a silly sight!

Celestial Paths Unraveled

Charting paths through space's thick fog,
Tangled in stardust like an overgrown dog.
I slipped on a comet, fell flat on my face,
Now I'm a star in an interstellar race!

My friends laughed hard as I drifted by,
On a rocket powered by blueberry pie.
With each bite I took, the engines would roar,
Launching me skyward, who knows what's in store?

Alien llamas popped up for a chat,
Wearing sunglasses and a sparkly hat.
They told me about their cosmic malls,
Where shopping carts float and nobody stalls.

I jot down notes with a crayon in hand,
Writing "Beware the galactic band."
As they strum their ukuleles so bright,
I'll dance among stars, till the morning light!

Notes from the Upper Realm

From the balcony of clouds, I scribble away,
Writing notes on the breeze, hoping they stay.
A hiccup from heaven, full of laughter and cheer,
As giggling rainbows spin in circles near.

The sun peeked in, teasing my hair,
Gave a wink and a nudge, "Hey, how's the air?"
A cloud floated by, with a fluffy demeanor,
Said, "Join me for tea—it'll make your day cleaner!"

I sipped on starlight, which tasted like fun,
Chatting with comets, oh what a run!
A grumpy old star rolled its twinkling eyes,
"Mundane down there, but oh how you rise!"

So I wrote of my antics in a playful scrawl,
Of silly balloons that refuse to fall.
In this upper realm of laughter and dreams,
I pen down the joy—or so it seems!

Beneath Heaven's Abode

In a field of daisies, I ponder my fate,
While ants form parades, they think they're so great.
Clouds look like puppies, just floating around,
And I'm here debating if squirrels wear crowns.

A bird sings a tune that's out of the key,
While I try to dance with glee in the breeze.
The sun plays a prank, it tickles my nose,
And I chase my own shadow, where it goes, who knows?

The grass whispers secrets, too silly to tell,
While I sip lemonade, oh isn't life swell?
A bumblebee buzzes, he's doing a jig,
I clap for his dance—he's a real little big.

A kite got tangled in a tree with a grin,
It flaps in defeat, but it's taking it in.
Oh, how I chuckle at nature's great show,
Beneath heaven's abode, there's always a flow.

Embrace of Infinite Horizons

Chasing my dreams on this broad open land,
I trip on a rock while making my stand.
The horizon keeps teasing me, saying, "Just run!"
While cows munch their grass, quite sure they've won.

A seagull squawks loud, thinks he owns the whole beach,
As I build a sandcastle, his reach seems to breach.
The waves laugh and tumble, playing tag with the shore,
While I try to keep up, oh, what's life for?

The sun takes a bow, it's setting with flair,
I smile at a crab that scuttles with care.
It peeks from its shell, oh shy little fellow,
As I wave at the stars, I feel so mellow.

In this embrace, I twirl with delight,
As fireflies dance, a flickering light.
A breeze gives me hugs, so sweet and divine,
Infinite horizons, where the laughter aligns.

The Meeting of Earth and Ether

The trees stand tall, wearing hats made of leaves,
While the wind whispers jokes that no one believes.
My feet in the mud, I hope for a shoe,
As daisies gossip, 'What's wrong with that dude?'

The mountains are watchful, with grins on their peaks,
And they grumble and rumble like old grumpy geeks.
Rocks on the path seem to giggle and trip,
I laugh with the daisies, take another dip.

A squirrel rides high on a bicycle made,
Of twigs and of dreams, in this forest parade.
I wave to the sky, with a wink and a cheer,
As clouds fluff my pillow, oh sweet atmosphere!

In this meeting spot, where the funny holds sway,
I dance with my dreams, while the sun fades away.
Under twinkling stars, we share gentle sighs,
Nature's comic timing, the universe's highs.

Whispering Ridges and Azure Dreams

On ridges so high, I hear whispers of fun,
While birds play charades, they've already won.
The sun takes a nap, slipping down the hill,
And giggles of shadows waltz on with a thrill.

The clouds form a train, puff puffs in the blue,
While I try to catch them, oh, what a zoo!
Each ridge has a secret, a laugh to unfold,
As the air fills with stories that never get old.

A picnic of ants, they feast on my crumbs,
I laugh at their party, all buzzing with hums.
An owl gives a hoot, like, "What's all the fuss?"
As I spin in circles, I'm one with the dust.

These azure dreams shimmer, they dance in the light,
As I chase all the giggles that flutter in flight.
Whispering ridges, full of laughter's sweet schemes,
Every step is a joy; I'm lost in the dreams.

A Tapestry of Celestial Views

I spotted a cat on a heavenly cloud,
With a crown on its head, it's feeling so proud.
It tossed down some stars, in a game of charades,
While giggling and pawing at glittery parades.

A squirrel in a suit tried to join in the fun,
But tripped on a moonbeam and landed - oh, run!
He hustled for acorns that floated on air,
While unicorns cheered with a whimsical flair.

The sun wore a hat made of daisies and light,
And painted the sky as it danced through the night.
A chorus of laughter arose from the breezes,
Mixing joy and wonder like autumnal leaves.

The stars raised a toast with their glimmering sips,
To the tales of brave critters with adventurous trips.
As the evening concluded, they settled their bets,
Only to wake up with some cosmic regrets.

The Threshold to Endless Blue

A penguin in flip-flops strutted on air,
Declaring a dance with a cloud for a pair.
He twirled and he twirled, with sunglasses so bright,
Singing songs of summer in the dead of night.

A giraffe poked its neck with a curious grin,
As the moon served up cookies from a wild tin.
They had snacks made of stardust and frozen delight,
And chatted about planets, from dusk until light.

A balloon tied to dreams bobbed up in the breeze,
Telling secrets of laughter amongst the tall trees.
It whispered of comets that zipped through the void,
And promised more giggles than ever enjoyed.

With shadows that danced and a comet's bright tail,
Each creature took flight, weaving stories in scale.
And when dawn approached with a yawning sky hue,
The laughter stayed locked in the hues of the blue.

Dancing Between Ground and Gaze

A squirrel in boots took a leap for the stars,
But landed in grass, still dreaming of cars.
He rolled on the floor, with his dreams in a swirl,
While bees buzzed a tune in a comical whirl.

A frog in a top hat jumped high for a snack,
And found that the cloud he adored had a crack.
It rolled out like jelly, with laughter so sweet,
As the sad, wobbling frog fell right to his feet.

The moon played a trumpet, too funky to miss,
While stars did the cha-cha in twinkling bliss.
With a wink of a comet and a giggle of sun,
The dance of the sky had finally begun!

As the daydreams took flight, in a colorful stream,
They discovered that nonsense was the best kind of dream.
So let's waltz with delight, in this cosmic parade,
And savor the laughter in the games that we've played.

The Stratospheric Secret

A chicken who flew with a feathered disguise,
Surveyed the strange world from high in the skies.
It plotted a route for a pie in the air,
To share it with friends who were dancing in flair.

With donuts that twirled like a merry-go-round,
And clouds that looked soft, like a plush velvet crown.
They floated on upside-down rainbows and dreams,
While giggles erupted like fizzy soda streams.

A beaver brought cookies, arranged in a line,
While fairies kept time with a tick and a twine.
They knitted together a quilt made of fun,
With mischief and wonder beneath the shining sun.

And when evening settled with stars in view,
They formed a brigade with a cheeky "Who knew?"
So from sweet little whispers to raucous delight,
It's clear that the stratosphere holds secrets so bright.

Embrace of the Heavens

In a town where birds wear shoes,
The clouds play hopscotch with the blues.
Cats ride bikes on the silver streets,
While the sun juggles with melting sweets.

A cow on stilts waves goodbye,
As squirrels dance and jump up high.
Rainbows get tangled in a kite,
As the stars laugh and twinkle bright.

A giraffe at the comic show,
Reads jokes that only cows would know.
The moon pulls faces at the sun,
In this land, we all have fun!

With dreams that bounce like rubber balls,
And ice cream cones as big as walls.
We twirl and spin in heaven's joy,
Squeezing laughter from every ploy.

Whispering Skies

In whispering winds, the jokes unfold,
With griffins sharing tales of old.
Clouds wear glasses to read the day,
While the sun takes a nap, dreaming away.

Tickling stars make wishes come true,
As elephants dance in brightly hued queue.
A snail zooms by on a skateboard ride,
While the moon grins wide, bursting with pride.

Colors mix like ice cream swirls,
As laughter flows with twirls and curls.
The rain giggles in splish-splashing tones,
While fish wear hats and toss funny bones.

An acorn tells tales of the tallest tree,
As the brook sings melodies, oh so free.
In this land, with whimsy we fly,
Counting the laughs beneath a spry sky.

In the Shadow of the Sky

I danced with clouds, quite a sight,
Tripped on a star, oh, what a fright!
My hat flew off into the breeze,
It landed right on top of some trees.

I waved to birds, they laughed real loud,
'Look at that human, oh so proud!'
I juggled raindrops, all in fun,
Till lightning struck, and I had to run.

The sun peeked out, gave me a wink,
Said, 'Life's too short, so grab a drink!'
I raised my cup, to the sky so bright,
Cheers to the mishaps, feeling just right.

So here I stand, with feet in the air,
While squirrels debate if I'm a bear.
Let's laugh together, in this high place,
As shadows dance with a silly face.

Paths to Eternity

In this maze of clouds, I lost my way,
Thought I'd zip by, but I went to play.
Tripping on sunbeams, oh what a scene,
I fell in a puddle, turned silver and green.

My GPS said, 'Turn left at the sun,'
But instead I found a cow that could run.
'Moo' she exclaimed, 'you're way off track!'
I laughed and followed her, no looking back.

A road made of rainbows stretched far and wide,
I met a pink llama, my new guide.
We skipped down the path with balloons in tow,
Seriously, who knew the sky was a show?

With giggles and hiccups, we journeyed bold,
The clouds hooted, 'This story's pure gold!'
Let's wander forever, dance to our glee,
Who knew paths to the void could be so free?

A Journey Upwards

I took a rocket made of cheese,
Amazed at its speed, I flew with ease.
Swarming with ants, I squeaked, 'Let's go!'
And up we soared, past the high and low!

We passed a moon with a smile so bright,
'Is that your spaceship? Oh, what a sight!'
I waved back at it, all shiny and round,
And cheese flung out, all over the ground.

Balloons tied to my socks flew near,
As I giggled at stars, they cheered with cheer.
'Look at that human, she thinks she can fly!'
But ups and downs, oh my, oh my.

In the depths of a comet, I found some glue,
I stuck it to dreams, let my craziness brew.
So here I am, in this marvelous spree,
Taking journeys off worlds, just silly me!

Heights of Wonder

On top of mountains, I found a chair,
It rocked back and forth, with a little flair.
I sipped on clouds, a sugary brew,
And watched the mountains fuss over who's who.

There's a squirrel band strumming a tune,
They said I should join, 'Come dance with the moon!'
But tripped on a stone, and down I went,
A tumble through daisies was my new intent.

With giggles and chuckles, the clouds joined in,
They painted my face with a whisk of wind.
I tickled the sun, it laughed back at me,
Said, 'You've got the knack for pure comedy!'

So here's to the heights, where laughs never cease,
Join in the fun, let your worries release.
With each silly moment, we soar ever high,
In the land of wonder, forever we fly.

www.ingramcontent.com/pod-product-compliance
Lightning Source LLC
Chambersburg PA
CBHW060139230426
43661CB00003B/485